Even Pink Duck Swims

Pina Hannan

Illustrated by Becky Hill

First published in Great Britain in 2017 by

Bannister Publications Ltd
118 Saltergate
Chesterfield
Derbyshire S40 1NG

Copyright © Pina Hannan

ISBN 978-1-909813-33-5

Pina Hannan asserts the moral right to be identified as the author of this work

A catalogue record for this book is available from the British Library

This book is sold subject to the condition that it shall not, by way of trade or otherwise, be lent, re-sold, hired out or otherwise circulated without the copyright holder's prior consent in any form of binding or cover other than that in which it is published and without a similar condition including this condition being imposed on the subsequent purchase.

All rights reserved. No part of this book may be reproduced or transmitted in any form or by any means, electronic or mechanical including photocopying, recording or by any information storage and retrieval system, without permission from the copyright holder, in writing.

Typeset by Escritor Design, Bournemouth

Printed and bound by SRP Ltd, Exeter

Logo by the late Patricia Hannan

Welcome to the Pink Duck series of books, taking children through the stages of learning to swim, following guidelines set by an approved pathway for learning to swim..

This is a factual story, with a hint of magic, based on four children as they progress through their swim journey.

The book is suitable for children aged four to seven years old. The aim, idea and end result of the story is to delight and enthuse them to want to learn to swim. The big prize is that once mastered, swimming is for life.

The author, Pina Hannan, is an ASA Level 3 Swimming Club Coach, ASA Level 2 Adult and Child Swimming Teacher, competition judge and timekeeper. She has spent many years teaching and coaching under the mentorship of the prestigious British Swimming Coach, Russ Barber. Based in the City of Sheffield, Russ has for many years produced successful and highly-regarded GB, European and Olympic swimmers at the City of Sheffield.

Pina has a great passion for teaching children to swim, and she does so in a way that has an easy appeal for youngsters. Her approach is to make learning fun, building confidence and good technique at a pace that suits each child.

I Wish I Could Swim…

One bright summer's day, two children called Ben and Danielle were out with their Mummy. As they stood on a grassy hill looking down at a pond, they saw four little ducks swimming along behind a big brown duck.

Ben said to his sister, "I wish I could swim like them," and Danielle replied, "Me too".

They both looked up at their Mummy and asked if they could learn to swim like the ducks. She smiled and told the children that when they got home she would sort out swimming lessons for them.

The First Swimming Lesson

It was time for Ben and Danielle's first swimming lesson. They were excited to see the pool and amazed to see how blue the water looked.

They quickly got into their swimming costumes and walked onto poolside to meet their teacher. She looked a kind lady, which made Ben and Danielle happy.

Then, next to the teacher, they saw a huge Pink Duck! It was sitting close to the water, ready to go for a swim. Ben and Danielle smiled as it reminded them of the Mummy duck they had seen on the pond.

The teacher told the children that that Pink Duck was magic. Ben and Danielle looked at each other. How could a pink duck be magic? What could the magic be?

The children sat at the side of the pool and the teacher helped them to put on flotation aids. There were two each, one that the teacher put on their backs and the other went around their body. The teacher said that this one was called a 'noodle'.

"Oh Yes," said Danielle. "It's just like noodles that we eat for tea!"

"That's right," said the teacher, "but these noodles stop you from wobbling and tipping over in the water."

Next, the teacher put Pink Duck into the water, and an amazing thing happened. The children couldn't believe their eyes when they saw that it could swim. It really was magic!

"Even Pink Duck can swim," laughed Ben.

The teacher showed Ben and Danielle how to enter the water. They felt quite safe because the flotation aids held them up, as they paddled along using their arms and legs.

The children splashed with their hands, trying to catch Pink Duck as she floated away. Just then, Ben noticed two other ducks in the water. One green and one red, and they were swimming towards Pink Duck. The teacher told the children that the little ducks were Pink Duck's babies.

The teacher had a raft that floated on water, and she asked Ben and Danielle to swim to Pink Duck and her babies, catch them and put them onto the raft.

After a lot of splashing and excitement, Ben reached Pink Duck first and put her on the raft. Danielle caught the two babies and put them on the raft, next to their Mummy.

"Now, hold on tight," said the teacher, and she pulled the raft along in the water. The children held on to it really tight and they loved being pulled along, especially when she went fast in the water.

Suddenly, one of the baby ducks fell off the raft, with a big Splash! Pink Duck looked upset to see her baby fall off, so Danielle let go of the raft and paddled with her arms and legs to reach the baby duck. When she got there, she then pushed it back towards its Mummy, and the teacher put the baby ducks back on the side of the pool.

Next, she let go of the raft, picked up another noodle from the side and said to the children, who were still holding on tightly, "Now, I'm going to make this noodle into a bridge. Kick your legs really fast in the water so you can push the raft along, and make it go under the bridge."

Ben and Danielle loved pushing and steering the raft, right under the Noodle Bridge. The teacher was very, very pleased with them… and so was Pink Duck!

The Little Red Boat

"Now," said the teacher, "this is my bag of special swimming toys… let me see what's in here…" and she took a red boat out of the toy bag and put it in the pool.

"The little red boat can follow us in the water," said the teacher. Danielle and Ben thought that would be good fun.

Suddenly they heard little splashes from behind them. The two other babies who had been sitting on the poolside decided to jump in the water.

"I think they want to be with their mummy again," said Danielle, "so they can join in the play."

"Oh look!" shouted Ben. "There's another duck in the teacher's special bag, and it's wriggling out!"

It was a little yellow duck. It jumped into the pool and climbed into the red boat.

"That's another of Pink Duck's babies," explained the teacher. "It's usually quite shy, but now it has seen all the fun, it wants to join in."

Off they all swam, the children the teacher, Pink Duck and all her babies. But they had not gone far when the teacher saw that the red boat was getting left behind.

"We'd better rest for a bit," said the teacher, and she took the children and Pink Duck back to the side of the pool where they could use the underwater steps to climb out of the water. There was a metal handrail to hold on to.

"You can take away your noodles now," said the teacher, "but we're keeping our floatation aids on your backs." As they did so, the red boat arrived at the steps, driven by a very tired little duck.

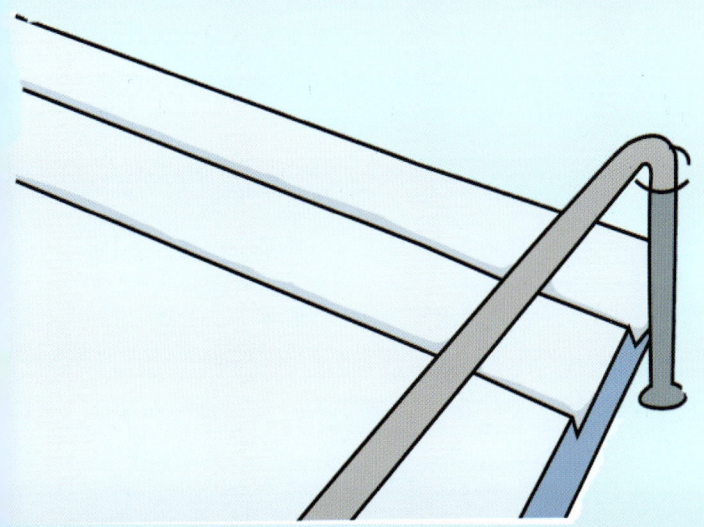

After a rest, the teacher showed the children how to jump into the water.

"You curl your toes around the edge of the pool, like this." She showed the children how to curl their toes… "and then JUMP!"

She jumped into the water and said, "Now you have a go."

Danielle curled her toes round the edge, being careful not to fall forwards, and then she jumped in. She splashed back to the steps, climbed out and sat next to Pink Duck.

Ben was a little frightened of jumping in by himself, so the teacher said, "Let's try a special jump, called a cuddle jump. You jump in and I'll catch you."

"I think I can do that," said Ben, feeling much braver now. He jumped and the teacher caught him. "Easy!" he shouted.

Ben decided to be brave on his next jump, and he jumped in all by himself towards the teacher, almost knocking her over.

Ben and Danielle were enjoyed their swimming lesson so much that they didn't hear their friends Eleanor and Laurie chatting loudly behind them. They looked around and Eleanor waved.

"It must be time for their lesson," said the teacher. "Time's up for today, Ben and Danielle."

The children were disappointed, but the teacher said, "Let's ask Pink Duck if you can come back next week for another lesson". They looked at her and saw that she was smiling, so they knew that she would want to see them again.

Eleanor was very excited because she remembered that the teacher had told her she could wear just the back flotation aid for this week's lesson. She did not need the noodle any more, which meant she would be able to go faster!

Pink Duck had jumped back into the water and was swimming away, so once the teacher had put on Laurie and Eleanor's flotation aids, they all entered the water to follow Pink Duck.

"Now, let's see if you can swim under the noodle bridge," said the teacher. She made a very low noodle bridge, much lower than they had ever tried before. "Pink Duck will show you how."

Pink Duck went under the bridge first, ducking her head down to look under the water. Then it was Eleanor's turn and she started to go through, but changed her mind because she didn't want to put her face in the water.

As she backed away she bumped into Laurie, who laughed. That made Eleanor decide to be really brave. She closed her eyes tight shut and swam under the bridge. Laurie followed, ducking his face down into the water.

"Well done children!" said the teacher.

Pink Duck then led the children back to the poolside.

"Time for the magic bag," said the teacher.

"What is it today?" asked the children, laughing at the thought of what might come out of the magic toy bag. It had all sorts of interesting things in it to make swimming lessons fun!

"Look at these," said the teacher, as two small floating toys appeared out of the bag. "We can put these in the water and blow on them to make them move along. Look, like this…" The teacher showed the children how to blow them along and how, by blowing very hard, you could flip them over.

Laurie was blowing very noisy bubbles, until it made him sneeze because the bubbles tickled his nose.

The teacher told them that if they could flip them over, they were blowing properly.

"Hey, look at my toy," shouted Laurie excitedly, " it's gone a different colour!". He had blown his toy right over and it was a different colour underneath.

Pink Duck noticed that Eleanor had secretly flipped hers over with her hand, but the teacher didn't notice. She gave both children a big clap.

Eleanor looked at Pink Duck who smiled at her as if to say, "I won't tell anyone what I saw you do with your hand. It's our secret".

"You did that very well," said the teacher. "Now let's try jumping into the water; this time without your flotation aids. Who's going to be first?"

"Me!", said Laurie and he jumped, going straight under the water, then back up again, laughing and splashing with his hands. He climbed out and sat on the side.

Eleanor was a bit worried because she didn't have her flotation aid on. "That's OK, Eleanor," said the teacher kindly, "Here, I'm in the water and I'll hold your hands as you jump."

Eleanor reached out to the teacher, who held her hand as she jumped in.

"Well done, Eleanor!"

She climbed out to join Laurie on the poolside. A moment later there were little splashing noises coming from the water. The children turned around and saw the red boat floating towards them, driven by one of the baby ducks.

"The baby duck looks tired," said Eleanor. "I'll get it." She stood up and then jumped in, ON HER OWN! She picked up the little baby duck from the red boat and put it back on the side of the pool.

"Thank you," said the teacher. "That was very brave Eleanor."

"Thank you," said the little duck, magically of course. "I was a bit tired."

Time had run out and the lesson was over. The teacher told the children how well they had done as she walked them back to their parents.

More Lessons at the Swimming Pool

It was swimming lesson day for Ben, Danielle, Eleanor and Laurie. When Ben and Danielle arrived at the swimming pool, the teacher and Pink Duck were waiting for them.

The children remembered to walk slowly on the wet poolside so they wouldn't slip. The teacher smiled and said, "Well done for remembering".

The teacher put on their flotation aids and asked them to enter the water. The children saw that she had put Pink Duck in the water with her yellow, green and red babies.

"Come on Ben and Danielle," said the teacher, "use your 'big arms' and 'fast legs' and let's see how fast you can go. See if you can catch Pink Duck and her three babies."

They followed Pink Duck and her babies to the steps. Danielle shouted, "We're swimming with the Mummy and baby ducks."

The children sat on the steps near the teacher's bag of toys. She took out three straws and gave the children a straw each keeping one for herself. Then she showed Ben and Danielle how to blow through the straw and make bubbles in the water.

Danielle had a go first and blew really hard making lots of bubbles.

Then it was Ben's turn but, oh dear, he got it wrong because he opened his mouth instead of blowing bubbles! "Oops!" said Ben.

"Have another go," said the teacher, and Ben blew hard, making great big bubbles in the water. The teacher said that the children could take the straws home to practise with their Mummy and Daddy.

The teacher then took Ben and Danielle for a walk in the pool, where it was shallow, to help them learn to balance. Danielle had to walk on tiptoe because the water came up to her neck, but Ben could walk properly.

Danielle was very careful, walking slowly through the water, Ben tried to race ahead and – whoops! He toppled over, but the teacher was there to pick him up. It didn't bother him at all, but Ben went back to the steps a bit slower than before.

The children sat together with their teacher. It was the end of the lesson. They gave Pink Duck a hug and said, "Bye bye, Pink Duck."

It was time for Eleanor and Laurie to have their swimming lesson. Laurie was excited because he had something special to show the teacher.

"Look what I can do," said Laurie, standing in the water. He bobbed down under the water and blew some massive bubbles. He jumped up, laughing with the others. "That's my trick for today," he said.

Eleanor was usually worried about going underwater, but today she was going to be brave. She put on her goggles and ducked down under the water, pressing her lips together to keep the water out. Then she blew, making a funny noise, and sending loads of little bubbles to the top of the water.

"I can see that you've both been practising at home," said the teacher. "Well done Eleanor and Laurie! I'm very proud of you both."

She rummaged in her magic toy bag and took out some sinking toys. "Not floating toys, today," she said, "these are sinking toys. Let's see if you can pick them off the bottom of the pool."

She let them sink to the bottom so that Laurie and Eleanor could fetch them. They didn't mind putting their heads under the water, now they'd dome so much practice. They picked up all the toys and blew lots of bubbles!

Laurie Swims without Flotation Aids

"Laurie," said the teacher, "I think you are ready to try swimming on your own."

Laurie gave a big happy grin and clapped his hands excitedly.

Eleanor sat on the poolside and put Pink Duck on her knee to watch.

"Swim to me," said the teacher, and Laurie set off, paddling forward as the teacher walked slowly backwards. He managed six paddles then stopped, while the teacher held him for a few seconds before turning him round.

"Now swim back to the side." Off he went, very fast this time, swimming with big front paddle arms and strong leg kicks. He reached the wall and climbed out.

Everybody in the pool, his Mummy, teacher and Eleanor all gave him a MASSIVE clap.

Laurie felt very proud of what he'd achieved. He had gone from needing flotation aids to swimming ON HIS OWN!

Time was up and the lesson was finished. Eleanor wanted to help the teacher put the toys away.

"Thank you," said the teacher, and then she spoke to all the children and their parents.

"Ben, Danielle, Eleanor and Laurie, I'm very pleased with what you have all learned in your swimming lessons. Your water skills are very good indeed. You have all earned special badges… like these."

And the teacher showed the children the badges that they had won. They couldn't wait to take them to school to show their teacher and friends!

Lots of Swimming on Holiday

After that, the children practised once a week with their teacher and once a week with their parents. Their water skills got even better, using their arms and legs and becoming more confident in the water.

It was soon school holiday time. Laurie was going away on holiday with his parents to a place that had a swimming pool. He was looking forward to swimming and playing in the pool – it would be extra fun now that he could swim a little.

He told his mummy and daddy that he was going to swim everyday so that he could get better and show his swimming teacher when he got back.

On the first day of his holiday, Laurie was walking round the pool in his swimming trunks, looking at the water, when a boy came rushing past.

"Ouch!" The boy slipped on the wet poolside and knocked Laurie into the swimming pool.

Laurie went straight under the water, then he came up, kicking his legs really hard, just as he had done in his swimming lessons. Then he swam to the side of the pool and climbed out. His parents had seen it happen and they rushed up to him and gave him a big hug. "Well done, Laurie," they said, "you did that fantastically well."

Laurie and his parents were very pleased that he had learnt to swim. "If you hadn't learned to swim," said his mummy, "you might easily have drowned."

Laurie decided that from that day he would become a really good swimmer. He would carry on having swimming lessons with his teacher until she thought that he was good enough to swim safely on his own.

The End